HE TURNED OUR CAPTIVITY

BY

GAYAH גיח

Unless otherwise noted, all scripture quotations are taken from King James Version, Apocrypha, The Book of Enoch, Jubilees and Jasher.

ISBN: 978-1-7340865-0-8

Library of Congress Control Number: 2019914809

Cover design by SOS Graphics

Published by G Publishing, LLC

Printed in the United States of America

Publisher Disclaimer: The views and opinions expressed in this book are solely those of the author.

Table of contents

When AHAYAH AHLAHAYAM turned again the captivity of Zion, *We were like them that dream.*

2Then was Our mouth filled with laughter, and Our tongue with singing: then said they among the heathen, AHAYAH AHLAHAYAM hath done great things for Them.

3AHAYAH AHLAHAYAM hath done great things for Us; *whereof* We are glad.

4Turn again Our captivity, O AHAYAH AHLAHAYAM, as the streams in the south.

5They that sow in tears shall reap in joy.

6He that goeth forth and weepeth, bearing precious seed, shall doubtless come again with rejoicing, bringing His sheaves *with Him.*

Psalm 126:1-6

Preface

Shalawam/Shalom! True and Rich Melanated Children of THE MOST HIGH POWER! My Hebrew Yisraelite Family!
I pray All Is Well With You! Family, it's time! Can You feel it? Can you see it? YASHA HA MASHAYACH IS COMING AND IS TURNING OUR CAPTIVITY BACK ONTO ALL OUR enemies; ALL OVER THE EARTH!

2 ESDRAS 6:9 Says: For esaw is the END OF THE WORLD and Yawachaab/Jacob be the beginning of it that followeth. I dont know about you but I KNOW it's time for True and Real Yisrael to rise up and begin to PRAISE OUR KING! FOR HIS DELIVERANCE IS NIGH AT HAND!

Have You ever wondered why Our Ancestor, Malak Dawad (King David), was so successful in His Walk with THE MOST HIGH?

For one, David FEARED THE MOST HIGH ENOUGH TO QUICKLY AND HUMBLE HIMSELF AND TRULY REPENT whenever He made a mistake. And number two, HE PRAISED THE MOST HIGH POWER FOR TARAH/TORAH AND THE PROPHETS CONTINUALLY! Psalm 119!

He also Said in Tahaliyam (Psalm) 34:1; "I WILL BARAK (BLESS) AHAYAH

5

AHLAHAYAM THE MOST HIGH POWER AT <u>ALL TIMES</u>. <u>HIS PRAISE</u> SHALL <u>CONTINUALLY</u> BE IN MY MOUTH."

Malak Dawad did not have time to fill His Mouth with the folly or madness of the wicked tribes/kingdoms around Us. He did not engage in nor condone Us fighting against One Another. Neither did Dawad waste His valuable time spewing put-downs of Our People but rather Honored and Esteemed ALL of Us Greatly; Men, Women and Children of Yisrael, in AHAYAH AHLAHAYAM! Malak Dawad held Our Ach's in High Regard to His Own flesh! HE Simply Reverentially Feared, Honored and Esteemed THE MOST HIGH with The Praises from His Mouth, His Mind, His Body, His Soul and His Rawach (Spirit)!

According to 2 Samuel 6:20 Dawad danced so hard before AHAYAH AHLAHAYAM for the return of The Ark of The Covenant to Our People, His Ephod and clothing fell off! His wife Michal wasn't too happy about that but it didn't stop Dawad from Honoring AHAYAH AHLAHAYAM! She lost her blessing of not being able to have children forever behind not having nor understanding the heart of worship and praise to THE MOST HIGH, too! And David and all The House Of Yisrael played before AHAYAH AHLAHAYAM on all manner of instruments made of fir wood, even on harps, and on psalteries, and on timbrels, and on cornets, and on cymbals 2 Samuel 6:5

> *And David danced before AHAYAH AHLAHAYAM with all His Might; and David was girded with a linen ephod. 2 Samuel 6:15 So David and all The House Of Yisrael brought up The Ark Of AHAYAH AHLAHAYAM with shouting, and with the sound of the trumpet. 2 Samuel 6:16*

> *And David said to Michal, It was before THE MOST HIGH, Who chose Me before Thy Father, and before all His House, to appoint Me Ruler over The People of AHAYAH AHLAHAYAM, over Yisrael: therefore will I play before AHAYAH AHLAHAYAM.*

MALAK/King DAWAD, HONORED AHAYAH'S LAWS, STATUTES AND COMMANDMENTS WITH HIS WHOLE HEART! THIS IS WHERE HIS PRAISE CAME FROM! This is the REAL Key to Success, Yisraelites.

All of this did Dawad do according to Scripture. What would Our lives be like today, if Our Ancestors Praised THE MOST HIGH FOR HIS EXCELLENT GREATNESS like Dawad instead of murmuring and complaining in the Wilderness? Dawad Honored THE MOST HIGH with <u>ALL</u> His Heart, Mind, Body, Soul and Strength, and it reflected in HIS PRAISE!

True Yisrael, We've been through TOO MUCH in this 400 plus years of captivity and slavery

*throughout the Diaspora across the Earth! WE
<u>REALLY</u> NEED TO PRAISE AHAYAH
AHLAHAYAM FOR HIS TURNING OUR
CAPTIVITY, RESTORATION OF REAL
Yisraelites, AND THE DESTRUCTION OF OUR
enemies!*

*PRAISE IS COMELY FOR THE UPRIGHT!
THAT'S US, AWAKENED
YASHARALAH/Yisrael!*

*LET'S COME TOGETHER WITH <u>ONE</u> SHOUT
OF PRAISE TO THE MOST HIGH AND
WATCH WHAT HE DOES IN THE EARTH
JUST FOR US! BECAUSE, <u>HE REALLY HAS
ALREADY TURNED OUR CAPTIVITY!
KAN! SO BE IT!</u>*

CHAPTER 1

א

THE TURN OF OUR CAPTIVITY

__If MY PEOPLE, Who ARE CALLED BY MY NAME, shall HUMBLE Themselves, and PRAY, and SEEK MY FACE, and TURN FROM Their wicked ways; THEN WILL I HEAR FROM HEAVEN, and WILL FORGIVE Their sin, and WILL HEAL Their Land.__
2 Chronicles 7:14

*IF **MY PEOPLE**...By now You should know **EXACTLY** Who AHAYAH'S **TRUE CHOSEN SEED/PEOPLE/CHILDREN** Be. By all the trouble alone, oppression and constant attack that plagues Our Community on a daily basis. You guessed it right. The **so-called Black People** a.k.a. **The Negro, scattered** all across the earth are The **True Scriptural Bloodline Decendants of Abaraham, Yisachaa/Isaac and Yawachaab/Jacob**. That's right. These **Melanated People Are The True Chosen Ones of THE ALL MIGHTY** the heathens have been mistreating all this time. AHAYAH had Our Identity stolen from Us during slavery by the sin-of-gog/synagauge of satan; a.k.a. so-called europeans who call themselves "jews" or-ISH. Revelations 2:9 Says to The True Seed: I know Thy works, and tribulation, and

9

poverty, (but Thou art rich) and *I know* the blasphemy of them which **say** they are "jews," and **are not**, but *are* the synagogue of satan. Revelations 3:9 also Says: Behold, I will make them of the synagogue of satan, which **say** they are jews, and **are not, but do lie**; behold, **I will make them** to come and worship before Thy Feet, and to **know** that **I have loved Thee**.

THE MOST HIGH IS **NOT** talking to the backwards insanity of christianity or ANY OTHER religious sect, cult or movement. HE IS STRICTLY TALKING TO HIS SPECIAL, CHOSEN, BEGOTTEN, SEED-THE Yisraelites. HE ALLOWED those "clubs," if you will, to be invented by the catholic "church" only for them to try to perpetually enslave, control and confuse the minds of Our People. Why? For stupidly rejecting HIM in The Wilderness after **HIS AWESOME AND OUTSTANDING ACTS** to deliver Us from the egyptians. (See Exodus.) Out of all 68 verses in Deuteronomy, with 1-14 being The Blessings for Obedience, 15 being the deal breaker, and 16-68 being the curses, Our Ancestors unfortunately **chose** the stipulation and curses of 15-68 for Us trying to be "like" the other nations around Us! They literally left **THE MOST HIGH** with no choice but to Curse, COMMAND, and Punish We, **HIS** TRUE PEOPLE! Deuteronomy 28:64 Says: And **THE MOST HIGH** shall scatter Thee among all people, from the one end of the earth even to the other; and there thou shalt serve **other** gods, **what neither thou nor thy fathers have known**, *even* **wood** (christianity) **and stone** (islam). Nothing more.

Nothing less.

Yaramiyah 17: 4 Says, *"And Thou, even Thyself, shalt discontinue from Thine Heritage THAT I GAVE THEE; and I WILL CAUSE Thee to serve Thine enemies in the land that Thou knowest not: for Ye have kindled a Fire in MINE Anger, that shall burn for ever."* Now, **HE** did not say We would discontinue from Our Heritage forever. **HE SAID** that **HIS** ANGER would Burn forever. Now, **HE IS waking HIS OWN PEOPLE up by HIS QADASH RAWACH (SET APART SPIRIT),** Messengers and Ambassadors Whom the world calls angels. There are heathens that would like to stop, slow down or hinder this Awakening but **THE MOST HIGH POWER AND ENERGY OF TRUE Yisrael CANNOT BE STOPPED, SLOWED DOWN NOR HINDERED**. IT'S JUST THAT SIMPLE.

*WE **ARE** THE **CALLED BY HIS NAME**. *"Now AHAYAH AHLAHAYAM had Said to Abram, Get Thee out of Thy country, and from Thy kindred, and from Thy father's house, to a land that I will shew Thee: And I WILL MAKE of Thee "A" GREAT NATION, and I WILL BLESS THEE, and make Thy Name Great; and Thou shalt be A Blessing: And I WILL BLESS them that Bless Thee, and curse him that curseth Thee: and in Thee shall all Families of the earth be blessed."* Think about it. Are **ALL** families of the earth blessed? No. As stated in My previous book, the catholic church changed certain wordings in Scripture to help hide Our True Identity making The Scripture *seem* "all inclusive," but it's not. It is **Our** History, Present and

11

Future Book. **We Are The only People** that fit the curses of Deuteronomy 28 for breaking AHAYAH AHLAHAYAM'S LAWS, STATUTES, AND COMMANDMENTS. We foolishly learned the idolatrous ways of the heathen *and* sadly, some Yisraelites taught the heathen to transgress worse than they already are/were! This is One of the key chapters of the Scripture that points straight to Us being The People of the **ENTIRE** Book. No matter who denies This Truth or desperately tries to change this fact, It Is What It Is. Or should I say We Be That/WHOSE We Be. Ex. 3:14.

Psalm 147:20 Says, "***HE hath not dealt so with ANY NATION: and as for His judgments, they have not known them. Praise Ye THE MOST HIGH POWER/ENERGY.***" Only True Yisraal.

Joel 2:23-29 Says, "***Be glad then, YE CHILDREN OF TAZAYAN, and REJOICE in AHAYAH Your AHLAHAYAM/POWER: for HE hath given you the former rain moderately, and HE WILL CAUSE to come down FOR YOU the rain, the former rain, and the latter rain in the first month. And the floors shall be full of wheat, and the vats shall overflow with wine and oil. And I WILL RESTORE TO YOU the (400+)YEARS that the locust hath eaten, the cankerworm, and the caterpillar, and the palmerworm, MY Great Army that I sent among You. And Ye shall eat in plenty, and be satisfied, and PRAISE THE NAME OF AHAYAH AHLAHAYAM YOUR POWER/ENERGY, that*** *hath dealt wondrously with YOU: and MY PEOPLE shall NEVER be ashamed. And Ye shall know that I am in the midst of Yisrael, and that I BE AHAYAH Your POWER, and NONE else: and MY PEOPLE shall NEVER be ashamed. And it shall come to pass afterward, that I WILL pour out MY Spirit upon all (Yisraelite) flesh; and Your Sons and Your Daughters shall Prophesy (not the tickle-your-ears prophets in the so-called church), Your old Men shall dream dreams, Your young men shall see visions: And also upon The Servants and upon The Handmaids in those days WILL I pour out MY RAWACH (Spirit.)"*

Humility is Key, Yisraelites. This is something Our enemies lack. TARAH/TORAH Teaches Us in Leviticus 26:40-42 Saying,"*If They shall confess Their iniquity, and the iniquity of Their Fathers, with Their trespass that They trespassed against ME, and that also They have walked contrary to ME; And that I also have walked contrary to Them, and have brought Them into the land of Their enemies; if then Their uncircumcised Hearts BE HUMBLED, and They then ACCEPT of the punishment of Their iniquity: THEN WILL I REMEMBER MY COVENANT with Yawachaab, and also MY Covenant with Yisaac, and also MY Covenant with Ahbaraham WILL I remember; and I WILL Remember The Land."*

Proverbs 15:33 Says, *"The fear of AHAYAH AHLAHAYAM IS the instruction of Wisdom; and BEFORE Honour is HUMILITY." "By HUMILITY and the (reverential) fear of THE ALMIGHTY are Riches, and Honour, and Life."* Says Proverbs 22:4. *"Humble Yourselves (True Yisrael) in the sight of THE MOST HIGH, and HE shall lift You up."* Says James 4:10.

"Serving AHAYAH AHLAHAYAM with ALL HUMILITY OF MIND, and with MANY tears, and temptations…" **AHAYAH AHLAHAYAM KNOWS** We know plenty about tears and temptations. NO other tribe/nation on earth knows more about these emotional drives than Yisraelites of the Diaspora. Colossians 2:23 Says, *"Those things have indeed a shew of Wisdom IN WILL Worship, and HUMILITY, and neglecting of the body: not in any honour to the satisfying of the flesh."* Another TARAH/TORAH Teaching on Humility is Deuteronomy 8:2-3 and It Reads as Follows; *"And Thou shalt remember all the way that AHAYAH AHLAHAYAM YOUR POWER led Thee these forty years in the wilderness, TO HUMBLE THEE, and TO PROVE THEE to KNOW what was in Thine Heart, whether Thou wouldest keep HIS Commandments, or no. And HE HUMBLED THEE, and suffered (allowed) Thee to hunger, and fed Thee with MANNA, that Thou knewest not, neither did Thy Fathers know; that HE might make Thee KNOW that "man doth not live by bread only, but by EVERY WORD" that proceedeth out of THE MOUTH of AHAYAH AHLAHAYAM doth man*

14

live." Sound familiar? Matthew 4:4, Luke 4:4.

*Because We Are **AHAYAH AHLAHAYAM'S TRUE** People and **PRAYER** Warriors, Prayer is something **ALL** Believing Yisraelites have The Right to take advantage of. Petitioning THE MOST HIGH POWER IS what MOST of Us do best! Most importantly, HE hears and answers Us if **WE HUMBLY HONOR HIM HIS WAY** with THE RIGHT HEART/MIND. 2 Chronicles 6:36-40 Says,*"If They (Yisraelites) sin against THEE, (for there is no Man that sinneth not,) and THOU be angry with Them, and deliver Them over before Their enemies, and They carry Them away captives to a land far off or near; Yet if They BETHINK Themselves in the land whither They are carried captive, and TURN and PRAY to THEE IN THE LAND OF THEIR captivity, Saying, We have sinned, We have done amiss, and have dealt wickedly; If They RETURN TO THEE with ALL THEIR HEART AND WITH ALL THEIR SOUL IN THE LAND OF THEIR captivity, whither They have carried Them captives, and PRAY TOWARD THEIR LAND, that THOU GAVEST to Their Fathers, and TOWARD THE CITY that THOU hast CHOSEN, and TOWARD THE HOUSE THAT I HAVE BUILT FOR THY NAME: THEN Hear THOU from The Heavens, even from THY Dwelling Place, Their PRAYER and Their Supplications, and MAINTAIN THEIR CAUSE, and FORGIVE THY PEOPLE Who have transgressed against THEE. Now, My POWER/ ENERGY, Let, I beseech THEE, THINE EYES be OPEN, and let THINE EARS BE ATTENTIVE TO*

THE PRAYER THAT IS MADE IN THIS PLACE." **Yisraelites**, We are to Pray without ceasing as 1 Thessalonians 5:17 Commands Us to!

*WE MUST SEEK AHAYAH AHLAHAYAM'S FACE NOW while We have the chance, Yisrael! Just as Isaiah 55:6-7 Commands Saying, "*SEEK YE AHAYAH AHLAHAYAM WHILE HE MAY BE FOUND, CALL YE UPON HIM WHILE HE IS NEAR: Let the wicked forsake his way, and the unrighteous man his thoughts: and let him RETURN BACK to AHAYAH, and HE WILL HAVE MERCY upon Him; and to Our POWER, for HE WILL ABUNDANTLY pardon.*" Time is of the essence, Yisraelite. While YASHA SON OF AHAYAH IS RIGHT in Saying in Matthew 24:35-37, "*Heaven and earth shall pass away, but MY WORDS shall not pass away. But OF THAT DAY AND HOUR KNOWETH NO MAN, no, not the angels of heaven, but MY FATHER ONLY. But as the days of Noah were, so shall also the coming of THE SON OF AHAYAH (Man) be.*" However, it is NOT Wise to tempt HIM! Ecclesiastes 12:1 Says, "*Remember NOW Thy CREATOR in the days of Thy youth, while the evil days come not, nor the years draw nigh, when Thou shalt say, I have no pleasure in them;*" True Yisrael, WE MUST SEEK THE MOST HIGH NOW **BEFORE** THE day of the wicked comes full force! How will or Can You *POSSIBLY* KNOW HIM THEN while all trouble is breaking lose?

*OUR PEOPLE MUST TURN BACK TO THE MOST HIGH; HIS LAWS THAT ARE **NOT**

DONE AWAY WITH, according to MATTHEW 5:17-19 and 1 John 5:2-3, **HIS** STATUTES AND **HIS** COMMANDMENTS **ARE STILL IN EFFECT** TO THIS DAY! **WE SIMPLY MUST, REPENT AND RETURN BACK TO THE MOST HIGH! EVEN TO OUR OWN LAND! GET OUT OF babylon WHILE YOU STILL CAN AND COME BACK HOME TO THE MOTHER LAND! AFRIKAH IS CALLING! EVEN N.E. AFRIKAH! HALALA! Deuteronomy 30:3-5; Ezekiel *11:17, 34:11-31, 36:24, verse 37, 37:21-27, *39:27-28; Yaramayah 23:3, 29:14, 30:3, 31:8, 32:37; Amos 9:14-15; Isaiah 11:11-16, 27:12-13, 43:5-6; Micah 7:12; Zephaniyah 3:19-20 Zachariyah 10:8-12; Psalm 106:47** IF WE DESIRE TO LIVE **AND** LIVE IN NEW YARASHALAYAM, WE **ABSOLUTELY MUST REPENT** AHAYAH AHLAHAYAM'S WAY! **We even have Our Own Feast Days, Y'all!** Leviticus 23! We mustn't any longer learn the vain ways and customs of the heathen! Yaramiyah 10:1-2. *"**Hear Ye THE WORD that AHAYAH AHLAHAYAM speaketh to You, O HOUSE OF (TRUE) Yisrael: Thus Saith AHAYAH AHLAHAYAM, LEARN NOT the way of the heathen, and BE NOT dismayed at the signs of heaven; for the heathen are dismayed at them**."* I don't know many TARAH Teaching Parents that will continue Blessing their Children Mercifully with wrong attitudes toward them. Do you? In fact, Scripture Deuteronomy 21:17-21 Says: *"**But He shall acknowledge the son of the hated for the firstborn, by giving Him a double portion of all that**"*

17

He hath: for He is the beginning of His Strength; the right of the firstborn is his. If a man have a stubborn and rebellious son, that will not obey the voice of His Father, or The Voice of His Mother, and that, when They have chastened him, will not hearken to Them: THEN shall his Father and His Mother lay hold on Him, and bring him out to The Elders of His TRIBE/city, and to The Gate of His Community/Place; And They shall Say to The Elders of His TRIBE/city, This Our son is stubborn and rebellious, he will not obey Our Voice; he is a glutton, and a drunkard. And all The Men of his TRIBE/city shall stone him with stones, that he die: so shalt Thou put evil away from among You; and ALL Yisrael shall hear, and fear." I am WAY more inclined to believe, since YASHA SHED **HIS BLOOD FOR US ALREADY, TRUE Yisrael**, if that son would **REPENT** to his Parents, he might be spared from that gruesome and painful death! Same with Us, True Yisrael!

*****THEN** WILL **AHAYAH AHLAHAYAM HEAR/SHAMA** from Shamiyam (Heaven) HE WILL **FORGIVE** OUR chaata (transgressions/"sin") and WILL **HEAL** OUR LAND!

TRUE Yisrael, WE NEED OUR LAND HEALED! HALALA!

CHAPTER 2

ב

DO IT AGAIN, MOST HIGH, DO IT AGAIN!

"At that time will I bring You AGAIN, even in the time that I GATHER YOU: for I WILL MAKE You A Name and A PRAISE among ALL People of the earth, WHEN I TURN BACK Your captivity before Your eyes, Saith AHAYAH" Zaphaniyah 3:20

I AM **TRULY** EXCITED ABOUT THE WORK OF **THE MOST HIGH! HE IS AND WILL GATHER US TOGETHER TO HIMSELF! HE WILL TURN** AND **IS TURNING** OUR captivity **AGAIN!** THIS TIME, **FOREVER RESTORING US BACK TO HIM AND TO OUR OWN LAND! HALALA!**

Just as AHAYAH AHLAHAYAM delivered Us from the first matazarim (egypt) **HE IS** DOING IT AGAIN AS I TYPE! ALL PRAISES!!

"I will not drive them out from before Thee in one year; lest The Land (YUDAH) become desolate, and the beast of the field multiply against Thee. BY LITTLE AND LITTLE I WILL DRIVE THEM OUT from before Thee, TIL THOU BE INCREASED, and inherit The Land." Exodus

23:29-30

Deuteronomy 7:21-23 Also States, *"Thou shalt NOT be affrighted at them: for AHAYAH Thy AHLAHAYAM/POWER IS among You, A MIGHTY FORCE and terrible. And AHAYAH Thy AHLAHAYAM/POWER WILL PUT OUT those nations before Thee BY LITTLE AND LITTLE: Thou mayest not consume them AT ONCE, lest the beasts of the field increase upon Thee. But AHAYAH AHLAHAYAM Thy STRENGTH/ ENERGY shall deliver them TO THEE, and shall DESTROY them with A MIGHTY DESTRUCTION, TIL THEY BE DESTROYED!"*

Exodus 14:13 Teaches Us, *"And Masha Said to The People, FEAR YE NOT! STAND STILL AND SEE THE SALVATION OF AHAYAH AHLAHAYAM! THAT HE WILL SHOW TO YOU TODAY: for the egyptians whom YE have seen to day, YE SHALL SEE them again NO MORE FOREVER!"*

These are the **POWERFULLY INSPIRING** and **ENCOURAGING** Scriptures the slave masters who stole Our Identity, did not want Us to read, learn or know for fear of YUDAH'S POWERFUL AND REVOLT! As We continue to Worship Our AHBA, HE WILL cause Our enemies to Worship Us! LET US MOVE AS A UNIT IN PRAISE, TRUE Yisrael!

CHAPTER 3

ג

NATURAL BORN LEADERSHIP SKILLS

BE WHO YOU ARE, YUDAH!

"Yudah, Thou Art He Whom Thy Brethren shall PRAISE: Thy Hand shall be in the neck of Thine enemies; Thy Father's Children shall bow down before Thee." YAHAWADAH/Yudah is a lion's whelp: from the prey, My son, Thou Art gone up: He stooped down, He couched as A Lion, and as an old Lion; who shall rouse Him up? The Sceptre shall not depart from YAHAWADAH/Yudah, nor a Lawgiver from between His Feet, TIL SHILOH come; and to HIM shall The Gathering of The People Be." Barashat/Genesis 49:8-10

The wicked flee when no man pursueth: but **The Righteous are BOLD AS A LION**. Proverbs 28:1. **YASHA IS THE LION OF YAHAWADAH/ YUDAH!** AHAYAH AHLAHAYAM HAS made it perfectly and abundantly clear that The Tribe of Yudah is HIS CHOICE Tribe of all 12 Tribes. We Are HIS Head Tribe. Almost all non-melaninated persons desire to be a so-called "Black" Person without having the actual problems or curses that

21

were placed upon Us by AHAYAH. Even Our Northern Kingdom Brothers and Sisters Who are still scattered throughout Afrikah, look down their nose at Us YAHUDAHITES in the Diaspora but want what they think is a benefit of what they call a so-called "Black/african american" in this land. When We, The Southern Kingdom, get fed up then The Northern Kingdom will wake up and get fed up. As We continue to WAKE UP, TURN BACK to valuing AHAYAH AHLAHAYAM'S LAWS, STATUTES AND COMMANDMENTS, Northern Kingdom will gain strength and confidence to join Us in the victorious battle to break the curse and call Our People OUT of **all** religions!AHAYAHIS IN CONTROL! HE WILL GATHER HIS CHILDREN TOGETHER BACK TO **HIMSELF!**

The word of AHAYAH AHLAHAYAM came again to Me, Saying, Moreover, Thou Son of Man, take Thee ONE STICK, and write upon it, For Yudah, and for the Children of Yisrael His Companions: then take another stick, and write upon it, For Yawasap/Yoseph, the stick of Ephraim and for ALL The House of Yisrael His Companions: And **join them one to another into one stick; and they shall become one in thine hand**.

And when The Children of Thy People shall speak to Thee, Saying, Wilt Thou not shew Us what Thou meanest by these?

Say to Them, Thus Saith AHAYAH AHLAHAYAM THY POWER; Behold, I will take the stick of Yoseph, that is in the hand of Ephraim, and The Tribes of Yisrael His Fellows,

and will put Them with Him, even with the stick of Yudah, and make them one stick, and they shall be one in mine hand.

And the sticks whereon Thou writest shall be in Thine Hand before Their Eyes.

And Say to Them, Thus Saith **AHAYAH AHLAHAYAM THY POWER;** Behold, I will take The children Of Yisrael from among the heathen, whither They be gone, and will gather Them on every side, and bring Them into Their Own Land: And I will make Them ONE NATION in The Land upon The Mountains Of Yisrael; and ONE KING shall be KING to Them ALL: and They shall be <u>NO MORE TWO NATIONS</u>, <u>neither shall they be divided into two kingdoms ANY MORE AT ALL.</u>

Neither shall They defile Themselves <u>ANY MORE</u> with Their idols, nor with their detestable things, nor with any of their transgressions: <u>BUT I WILL SAVE THEM OUT OF ALL THEIR dwelling places</u>, wherein They have sinned, and <u>WILL CLEANSE THEM</u>: so shall They be MY PEOPLE, and I WILL BE THEIR POWER/ ENERGY!" HALALA!! TO **AHAYAH AHLAHAYAM** BE ALL THE ESTEEM!!!

One of the things Our People need to understand is that **the curses of chaayan/cain who are hamites, are _NOT_ the same curses that were upon The Yisraelites**. Both melanated People but of 2 separate Tribes.

Get your passports, your plane tickets, your popcorn

and favorite drinks ready, Y'all! 'Cause the firework curses that were on Our People, The Hebrews, Yisraelites, a.k.a. Negro/Black People, are now being reversed back upon Our enemies and the effects are showing! KAN! HALALA! All those billions and trillions of dollars each year is spent in babylon amerika and the land of Yisrael, wasted to try and keep Northern and Southern Kingdoms separate because as stated in Mark 3:25, "A House divided against itself cannot stand," will soon prove to be vain, futile, frivolous against Us but devastatingly catastrophic for them to their own demise. Revelation 13:10 Says: **he that leadeth into captivity, shall also go into captivity. he that killeth with the sword, MUST be killed with the sword. Herein is the Patience and the Faith of The Saints.**

That being said, **MALAK YASHA HA MASHAYACH** TAZABAATH (CAPTAIN OF HOST/ARMIES) AHLAHAYAM IS COMING TO **FIERCELY** TAKE BACK AND CLEANS HIS LAND Yisrael IN N.E. AFRIKAH, FROM THE gentile heathens currently "occupying" it. HE WILL REPAY THEM TO THEIR FACE as Spoken of in Deuteronomy 7:10, RESTORE AND PUT **HIS MASHAPACHAA/ FAMILY** BACK TOGETHER AGAIN **PERMANENTLY, FOREVER AND HE WILL USE YUDAH TO BRING IT OUT! ALL PRAISES!!** We Sisters and Brothers will NEVER be divided again. We Will **ALL** Have **ONE** SHAPATHA/ LAWGIVER and We will ALL live under AHAYAH'S LAW! *Ye shall have One manner of Law, as well for the stranger, as for One*

24

of Your Own Tribe (Country): for I am AHAYAH AHLAHAYAM your POWER. Leviticus 24:22

One Law and ONE manner shall be for You, and for the stranger that sojourneth with You.
Numbers 15:16

QAM YAHAWADAH! RISE YUDAH! QAM YASHARALAH! RISE Yisrael!

PRAISE IS WHAT WE DO AND DELIVERANCE OF THE MOST HIGHS REAL PEOPLE; THE RIGHTEOUS WHO CALL ON HIM OUT OF A PURE HEART, IS WHAT AHAYAH REQUIRES! KAN!

CHAPTER 4

ㄱ

OUR EYES ARE ON YOU, AHAYAH!

One of My FAVORITE Records of THE MOST HIGH **coming through for HIS People** is found in 2nd Chronicles 20:12-30. It reads as follows:

"O AHAYAH Our AHLAHAYAM POWER/ENERGY/STRENGTH, wilt THOU not judge them? for We have no might against this great company that cometh against Us; neither know We what to do: "BUT OUR EYES ARE UPON YOU."

And ALL Yudah stood before AHAYAH AHLAHAYAM, with Their Little Ones, Their Wives, and Their Children.

Then upon Yahazial the Son of Zachariyah, the Son of Banaiyah, the Son of Yaial, the Son of Mattaniyah, A Levite of the Sons of Asaph, came THE RAWACH (Spirit) of AHAYAH in the midst of the congregation;

And He Said, Hearken Ye, ALL YAHAWADAH/YUDAH, AND Ye Inhabitants of Yarashaliyam (Yerusalem,) and Thou King Yahoshaphat, Thus Saith AHAYAH AHLAHAYAM to You, BE NOT AFRAID NOR

DISMAYED by reason of this great multitude; FOR THE BATTLE IS NOT YOURS, BUT AHAYAH'S.

To morrow go Ye down against them: behold, they come up by the cliff of Ziz; and ye shall find them at the end of the brook, before the wilderness of Yarual.

Ye shall not need to fight in this battle: set Yourselves, stand Ye still, and SEE The Salvation of AHAYAH with You, O Yudah and Yerusalem: FEAR NOT, NOR BE DISMAYED; to morrow go out against them: for AHAYAH AHLAHAYAM WILL BE WITH YOU.

And Yahoshaphat bowed His Head with His Face to the ground: and ALL Yudah and The Inhabitants of Yarawashaliyam fell before THE MOST HIGH, WORSHIPING YAH.

And The Levites (HAITIANS), of The Children of The Kohathites, and of The Children of The Korhites, STOOD UP TO PRAISE AHAYAH AHLAHAYAM ENERGY/POWER of Yisrael with A LOUD VOICE ON HIGH.

And They rose early in the morning, and went forth into the wilderness of Takawah: and AS THEY WENT FORTH, Yehoshaphat stood and Said, Hear Me, O Yudah, AND Ye Inhabitants of Yerusalem; BELIEVE IN AHAYAH

27

AHLAHAYAM   *YOUR POWER/ENERGY/STRENGTH, SO SHALL YE BE ESTABLISHED; BELIEVE "HIS (REAL AND TRUE Yisraelite) Prophets" (NOT the ones representing the religious money-making so-called "church" organization), SO SHALL YE PROSPER.*

And when He had consulted with The People, He appointed Singers to AHAYAH AHLAHAYAM, and that should PRAISE THE BEAUTY OF (BEING) QADASH (holiness), as They went out before The Army, and to Say, Praise AHAYAH AHLAHAYAM; for HIS CHAANAH (mercy) Endureth FOREVER.

And when They BEGAN to SING AND TO PRAISE, AHAYAH AHLAHAYAM SET AMBUSHMENTS against the children of ammon, moab, and mount seir, that were come against Yudah; and they were smitten.

For the children of ammon and moab stood up against the inhabitants of mount seir, utterly to slay and destroy them: and when they had made an end of the inhabitants of seir, every one helped to destroy another.

And when Yudah came toward the watch tower in the wilderness, they looked to the multitude, and, behold, they were dead bodies fallen to the earth, and NONE escaped.

And when Yahoshaphat and His People came to take away the spoil of them, They found among them in abundance both riches with the dead bodies, and precious jewels, that They stripped off for Themselves, more than they could carry away: and They were THREE DAYS IN GATHERING OF THE SPOIL, IT WAS SO MUCH.

And on the fourth day They assembled Themselves in the valley of Barachah; for There They BARAK (BLESSED) AHAYAH: therefore the name of the same place was called, The Valley Of BARACHAAH, to this day.

Then They returned, every man of Yudah and Yarashaliyam, and Yahoshaphat in the forefront of Them, TO GO AGAIN to Yarashaliyam WITH JOY; FOR AHAYAH AHLAHAYAM AHLAHAYAM HAD MADE THEM REJOICE OVER THEIR enemies. KAN!

And they came to Yarashaliyam with psalteries and harps and YAWABALAH/SHAWAPARA/ trumpets to THE HOUSE OF AHAYAH AHLAHAYAM.

And THE FEAR OF AHAYAH AHLAHAYAM was on ALL the kingdoms of those countries, when they had HEARD that YASHAYAH TAZABAAT fought against the enemies of Yisrael.

29

So the realm of Yahoshaphat WAS QUIET: for His POWER GAVE HIM REST ROUND ABOUT.

The same enemies after Us then are the same ones coming against Us today but THE MOST HIGH **assured** Us **HE WILL RESCUE US FROM THEM "ALL" . . . "AGAIN" . . . "FINALLY", "FOREVER" AND FOR OUR GOOD**! KAN! SO BE IT! HALALA!

I TELL YOU, Yisraelite, PRAISE IS COMELY FOR THE UPRIGHT!

KAN!

CHAPTER 5

ה

AHAYAH AHLAHAYAM WILL

OVERTURN, OVERTURN, OVERTURN IT!

"I WILL Overturn, Overturn, Overturn, It: and It shall be NO MORE, TIL HE come WHOSE RIGHT IT IS; and I WILL GIVE It HIM."
Ezekiel 21:27

As Hebrew Yisraelites We go through more problems for a short while now than the average person. Why? Simply because We are **HIS**! For **THE NAME OF MASHAYACH! We Truly Are THE MOST HIGH'S** True, Chosen, Melanated, Bloodline Seed of Abaraham, Yisaakh, and Yawachaab. We Are HIS TRUE Shamites! We truly are held to the Higher Standard of TARAH/TORAH BECAUSE WE ARE The True Light and Salt of the earth for the other tribes/nations to see. Therefore, AHAYAH Helps Us to meet HIS STANDARD for this purpose. *"And YASHA ANSWERED and Said TO Them, Take heed that NO MAN deceive You!"* *Matthew 24:4*

"But HE Answered and Said, I am not sent ONLY to THE LOST SHEEP OF THE HOUSE OF Yisrael." Matthew 15:24

As a result of this, the heathen nations, with that proud, entitled spirit they reek of, through religion and their follytics, really try to test the boundaries and limits of **THE MOST HIGH** by trying to bogart their way into any spaces Yisraelites are in and they are not welcome! with, through and for HIS People. They have taken, stolen, and destroyed much in Our Community and the world so NOW, **THE MOST HIGH IS** Saying, "Enough!" THE ALL MIGHTY ONE Promises Us through **HIS** Prophet Yaramiyah 16:17-18 and 17:17-18 *"For MINE EYES ARE upon ALL their ways: they are NOT hid from MY FACE, neither is their iniquity hid from MINE EYES.*

And FIRST I WILL RECOMPENSE their iniquity AND their sin DOUBLE; BECAUSE they have defiled MY LAND, they have filled MINE INHERITANCE with the carcases of their detestable and abominable things.

O AHAYAH AHLAHAYAM, My STRENGTH/ENERGY/POWER, and My FORTRESS, and My REFUGE in the day of affliction, the (heathen) gentiles shall come to THEE from the ends of the earth, and shall say, Surely our fathers have INHERITED LIES, vanity, and things wherein there is NO profit.

BE NOT A TERROR TO ME: THOU ART MY HOPE in the day of evil.

Let "them" be confounded that persecute Me, BUT LET NOT ME be confounded: let "them" be dismayed, BUT LET NOT ME be dismayed:

BRING UPON "them" the day of evil, and
DESTROY "them" WITH DOUBLE
DESTRUCTION."

Let's face it, Real Yisrael, sadly and shamefully, Our People messed up by disHonoring or shall I say, disin' **Our ONE TRUE POWER AND KING!** Nevertheless, HE has NOT cast **We HIS TRUE People** off and WILL **YET** CHOOSE US AGAIN! **TRUE REPENTANCE IS KEY** FOR OUR **DELIVERANCE, SALVATION AND RESCUE.** WE MUST GET DOWN ON OUR KNEES AND FACES AND **REPENT TO THE MOST HIGH! HE DESERVES OUR LOVE, LOYALTY, HUMILITY AND SERVICE! HE ALONE IS WORTHY TO BE PRAISED!!** **NOT** a man who sets himself up as a so-called religious power or ruler. Those have PROVEN to hate **THE MOST HIGH, HIS TRUE PEOPLE AND HIS CREATION** by using false humility and false "peace" to destroy EVERYTHING AHAYAH AHLAHAYAM Created. It TRULY makes Me wince and grieved inside to say with trembling that this is how 2/3rds of Our People will be destroyed. They will be too comfortable in their lust of the flesh, lust of the eye, and the pride of life to wake up in time. They won't listen or take heed as They should; and so, will absolutely perish with and be named among the wicked. I sure hate that for you! **PLEASE**, My Dearly Beloved Brothas and Sistas of the Diaspora that are still sleeping or on the fence about This Truth, **wake up soon, and VERY SOON. LETS LOVE EACH OTHER AGAIN AS WE "ALL" WAYS DID before its too late.**

However, I do pray You will wake up since YASHA/AHAYAH AHLAHAYAM AHLAHAYAMSHI/ YAHUSHA HA MASHAYACH (WHOM the world ignorantly calls j.c.) **BECAME Our ETERNAL OATH** to AHAYAH**FOR** Us by the shedding of HIS BLOOD after Our People had HIM beaten and murdered by our own people by way of the heathens on a tree. You see, Real Yisrael, since HE rose from the dead 3 days later by THE POWER OF RAWACH QADASH and is now seated at the right HAND of Our AHBA... well, actually, I Believe HE IS standing at THE GATE waiting for the moment to come rescue Us! ALL PRAISES! **HE IS ALIVE AND WELL! HE NOW LIVES IN US! WAKE UP AND COME OUT FROM AMONG THEM AND PARTAKE NOT OF THE UNCLEAN THING!! PLEASE,** TRUE AND VERY REAL Yisrael! **LET'S REPENT AND OBEY AHAYAH'S COMMANDMENTS!** THEY ARE **NOT** DONE AWAY WITH AS TOLD BY THE so-called church! THEN THERE WOULD BE LAWLESSNESS AND POLLUTION OF **OUR PEOPLE; WHOM THE LAW WAS GIVEN TO IN THE FIRST PLACE,** GET IT? LET'S PRAISE AND WORSHIP **OUR TRUE KING** AND POWER TOGETHER! THEN, LET'S WATCH HIM FIGHT AND MOVE MOUNTAINS **FOR US** AS A PEOPLE! HIS PEOPLE! KAN!

Yachaanan 4:22-24 shows Us where YASHA Says to a **Dark-skinned, Northern Kingdom Yisraelite Woman** who lived *in* Samaria, Who, as all Northern Kingdom did, hence the split from Our Southern

Kingdom, refused to accept Shalaman's Son Rahaboam as King of Yasharalah,

*"**Ye worship Ye know not WHAT: WE KNOW WHAT WE WORSHIP: FOR SALVATION IS OF YAHAWADAH/YUDAH (A.K.A.) THE (REAL) so-called "Jews." But the hour cometh, and NOW IS, WHEN THE TRUE WORSHIPERS SHALL WORSHIP HA AHBA (The Father) in RAWACH (Spirit) AND in AHMANATHA (Truth): for HA AHBA (The Father) SEEKETH SUCH TO WORSHIP HIM. ***"AHAYAH AHLAHAYAM IS A RAWACH (Spirit): and THEY that WORSHIP HIM MUST WORSHIP HIM IN RAWACH (SPIRIT) AND IN AHMANATHA (TRUTH)."***

THIS IS US, SO-CALLED NEGRO/BLACK PEOPLE SCATTERED AND SOON TO BE FULLY GATHERED BY THE MOST HIGH ACROSS THE EARTH!! Notice how **WE ARE the Real, True Singers and Worshipers of the earth** everyone wants to imitate, emulate and be entertained by? Where do You think the meaning and term "Soul Music" comes from? Why? Who labeled it as such? Think about it. Our Musical Voices and Dancing Skills were **NEVER** intended for soulless "mankind's" pleasure or enjoyment. ONLY for AHAYAH'S **HONOR!** shatans seed know this. Remember, the deceiver was the most beautiful messenger or ambassador for **THE MOST HIGH**. From what I've learned, he was literally created with musical instruments within his physical being! How beautiful is that?! Nevertheless, he let that go to his head and got kicked out of Shamiyam by AHAYAH

THE MOST HIGH POWER taking 1/3 of the messengers with him. Now, for the short time being, the earth is stuck with him and his deception through his wicked heathen seed! *"**Therefore rejoice, Ye heavens, and Ye that dwell in Them. Woe to the inhabiters of The Earth and of The Sea! for ha shatan is come down to you, having great wrath, BECAUSE he KNOWETH THAT he HATH BUT A SHORT TIME!"*** Revelation 12:12** Notice how We Are A wholesome and modest set apart People to AHAYAH but the wicked singers and "entertainers" are anything but! Absolute opposite of AHAYAH!

Tell Me, who's behind that twisted wickedness for cumbersome money, burdensome fame and exhausting, controlled and costly fortune? What's at the end of that short-lived rope? Ha shatan to collect on that blood contract you signed. With AHAYAH, no one has to die or be sacrificed for HIS BLESSINGS since YASHA paid it all! Proverbs 10:22 Says of The Real Yisraelite Who has **The Real Blessing** of Ahbaraham and Masha from **THE MOST HIGH POWER** UPON US, *"**THE BLESSING OF THE MOST HIGH, IT maketh Rich, and HE addeth NO sorrow with IT.**"* KAN! This is one of the MANY POWERFUL reasons We Honor and Praise AHAYAH. Not only for what We are able to receive from HIM AS his True Children but for WHO HE IS THAT PROVIDES FOR US! Because of THE WARRIOR, LIFE GIVER, WAY MAKER, HEALER, RIGHTEOUS, RULER, LAWYER, JUDGE, PROTECTOR, GUIDE BATTLE AXE, POWER, ENERGY, STRENGTH,

SHALAWAM GIVER, AHBA We True awakened Yisraelites can Trust and HONOR HIM!

CHAPTER 6

I

FROM SUNRISE TO SUNDOWN

"From the rising of the sun to the going down of the same AHAYAH AHLAHAYAM AHLAHAYAM'S NAME IS TO BE PRAISED!"
Psalm 113:3

"And it came to pass, when Masha held up His hand, that Yisrael prevailed: and when He let down His hand, amalek prevailed. But Masha's hands were heavy; and they took a stone, and put it under Him, and He sat thereon; and Aaron and Hawarah/Hur stayed up His hands, the one on the one side, and the other on the other side; and His hands were steady til the going down of the sun. And Yashawah discomfited amalek and his people with the edge of the sword." Exodus 17:11-13

Did You know Masha was a songwriter? That's The Yisraelite in Him! *Then Sang Masha and the Children Of Yisrael THIS SONG TO AHAYAH AHLAHAYAM, and Spake, Saying, I WILL SING to AHAYAH AHLAHAYAM, for HE hath Triumphed gloriously: the horse and his rider hath HE thrown into the sea. AHAYAH AHLAHAYAM*

IS MY STRENGTH AND SONG, and HE IS become MY Salvation: HE IS MY POWER, and I will PREPARE HIM An Habitation; My father's POWER, and I will exalt HIM. AHAYAH AHLAHAYAM IS A MAN OF WAR: AHAYAH AHLAHAYAM IS HIS NAME! Exodus 15:1-3.

These scripture go hand in hand to Me. Let's face it, Yisrael had jealous and envious enemies that needed to be subdued. Period. I'm talking about being eradicated permanently. Our People were thirsty, that led to sadly and wrongfully complaining in a vulnerable place against AHAYAH through HIS Servant Masha. Masha was instructed by AHAYAH AHLAHAYAM to strike the Rock in the wilderness of Rephidim called Massah and Marabah (Place of Testing and strife) so that Our Ancestors could have and drink water to quench their thirst and that HIS POWER would be Greatly Demonstrated. When all of a sudden, They are approached by amalekites a.k.a. fake jews called kazarians today, to fight and strive against Us Real Yisraelites. Nothing new under the sun, right? Go figure. Well, as long as Masha's Hands were extended to AHAYAH AHLAHAYAM, Our People succeeded against Our enemies; but, when he let His Arms down due to heaviness, We began to lose. Well, as Our Ach's should still do today, Yashawah and Hawarah saw the need of The Man of AHAYAH, met that need by coming alongside Him with a stone for Him to rest on and each Ach held up Masha's Arms one on each side. All three Kings did their part for the common good of Our Nation and AHAYAH AHLAHAYAM HONORED Our National Teamwork! And guess what? AHAYAH GAVE US THE VICTORY AND WE WON THE WAR! HALALA! Can you imagine what that day would have looked like if they hadve been bickering and fighting amongst One Another instead of Our enemies? Or letting Masha carry His burden alone? "Well, that's how You do it over there and this is how We do it over here!" NO! AHAYAH FORBID! ACHAAD! ALL PRAISES TO THE MOST HIGH POWER AHBA AHAYAH! Our Yisraelite Kings and Priests were Mature enough to care for the Business of AHAYAH AHLAHAYAM'S TRUE PEOPLE AS A WHOLE in Worship, by knowing who the True enemies are, fight against *them* and prevail by THE POWER AND ENERGY OF OUR AHBA AHAYAH! KAN! HALALA!!

I'm sure Our Sister's were home Caring for Our Young, Covering, Wailing, Praising and lifting up on HIGH Our Men/King's of The Earth to THE MOST HIGH in Prayer! Not bashing them, putting them down or forcing them to strange women with their nagging words whenever they got home from the battle! I'm sure there was *lots* of celebrating in a BIG way as well as Yisraelite Baby making as AHAYAH Commanded Us, True Yisrael, when HE SAID, "*And AHAYAH AHLAHAYAM BLESSED Them, and AHAYAH AHLAHAYAM Said to Them, Be fruitful, and Multiply, and Replenish The Earth, and Subdue It...*" in Barashat/Genesis 1:28; "*And You, be Ye Fruitful, and Multiply; bring forth ABUNDANTLY on The Earth, and Multiply Therein.*" Barashat 9:7; "*And AHAYAH Almighty Bless Thee, and make Thee Fruitful, and Multiply*

40

Thee, that Thou mayest be A Multitude Of People" Barashat 28:3; *"__And Said to Me, Behold, I WILL Make Thee Fruitful, and Multiply Thee, and I WILL Make of Thee A Multitude of People; and WILL give this land to Thy Seed after Thee for an EVERLASTING Possession.__"* Barashat 48:4. The people spoken against in Revelation 2:9 and 3:9, pretending to be Yisrael, currently occupying land that is part of *Our* True Inheritance called by Our Rich Melanin Ancestor Yisrael today, but not for long according to AHAYAH, absolutely cannot claim these Scriptures. As you read, their birthrate is declining and diminishing every second of the day. ALL PRAISES! Proven facts. Just look it up and do your own research!

Now, I know there was lots of Feasting in Chaanah (A Graceful, Safe and Beautiful Place) to AHAYAH in Thanksgiving among Our People that day and many others thereafter! HALALA! We *must* learn how to celebrate and honor each others Victories, Yisrael. Like Our Achwath in Luke 15:8-9, *"__Either what (Yisraelite) Woman having ten pieces of silver, if She lose one piece, doth not light a candle, and sweep the house, and seek diligently till She find it? And when She hath found it, She calleth Her Friends and Her Neighbours together, saying, "REJOICE WITH ME; for I have found the piece that I had lost.__"*

REJOICING IS WHAT WE DO, TRUE Yisrael! __NOBODY__ KNOWS HOW TO PAR-TAY LIKE THE TRUE AND REAL MELANINATED Yisraelites! __NOBODAY__! KAN! In fact, The Real and Festive Party don't start TIL We get there! KAN! We Are The **ONLY** People that bring **LIFE** to The Party! ALL PRAISES TO RAWACH QADASH!!

As HIS Peculiar People, not in a religious way either, let Us also Thank HIM in advanced, True Yisrael! We simply *MUST* <u>**REMEMBER**</u> to **Pray**, **Fast**, **Worship with Thanksgiving** and **Praise** Our HEAVENLY AHBA AHAYAH for the Victories HE Works in ALL Our Awakened Yisraelite Lives, always! No matter how large or small. With THE MOST HIGH AS OUR ONE TRUE POWER, THERE IS NO SUCH THING AS SMALL BLESSINGS. Those Victories that may seem small, **really are** <u>GINORMOUS</u> <u>MIRACLES</u>! KAN!! **WE PRAISE YOU AND THANK YOU IN ADVANCE, AHBA AHAYAH AHLAHAYAM, FOR <u>YOUR CHAANAH/BEAUTIFUL GRACE,</u> <u>MERCY</u> AND <u>MANY</u> BLESSINGS! *AND...* BECAUSE YOU'VE TURNED OUR CAPTIVITY!**

ᴛ

AHAYAH'S MERCY ENDURES FOREVER!

O Give Thanks to AHAYAH AHLAHAYAM AHLAHAYAM; for HE IS Good: for HIS /CHAANAH (mercy) endureth for EVER.
Psalm 136:1

I think this chapter is one of the most perfect and encompassing displays of Praise, Worship, Honor and Adoration to THE MOST HIGH for ALL HIS POWERFUL, MIGHTY and RIGHTEOUS DELIVERANCE and ACTS performed and executed for HIS TRUE CHILDREN OF Yisrael in all the books of Psalms combined! It demonstrates HIS Mercy for Us as well! That alone is nothing to sneer at nor take lightly or for granted.

O give thanks to AHAYAH AHLAHAYAM; for HE is good: for HIS Mercy endureth for ever.

2 O give thanks to THE POWER of powers: for HIS Mercy endureth for ever.

Psalm 136:1-26

This whole chapter sums up Our Past and Present Deliverance of AHAYAH AHLAHAYAM'S TRUE PEOPLE! This is A Great self-explanatory

Testimony and demonstration of AHAYAH'S GOODNESS AND CARE for Us as HIS OWN AHWAMAH/Yisraelite Tribe.

HALALA! THAWADAH AHAYAH AHLAHAYAM! KA LA CHAASADA!

HALALA! THANK YOU AHAYAH AHLAHAYAM FOR YOUR MERCY ENDURES FOREVER!

CHAPTER 8

ח

THE POWER OF TESTIMONY

And They (True Hebrew Yisraelites) *OVERCAME* him by THE BLOOD OF THE LAMB, and BY THE WORD OF THEIR TESTIMONY; Revelation 12:11

It has often been said that One cannot have the testimony without the test. I can personally tell You how True this claim is. Now, I can also tell You that, "***There hath no temptation taken You but such as is common to man: but AHAYAH IS FAITHFUL, WHO will NOT suffer You to be tempted above that Ye are able; but WILL with the temptation also make a way to escape, that Ye may be able to bear it.***" 1 Corinthians 10:13.

If I could equate a song to this chapter, it would be, "YOU'VE Done **SO MUCH** For Me, I Cannot Tell It All!" HALALA! Where to begin?

AHAYAH AHLAHAYAM IS AWESOME! **THERE IS NO ONE LIKE HIM!** The Scriptures, from Barashat/ genesis-*revelation plus all The Other Books that were removed from Our Scripture during Slavery, by the roman catholic church, give HUGE TESTIMONY of AHAYAH AHLAHAYAM WA*

*QADASH RAWACH BA(IN) HA(THE) SHAM(NAME) YASHA HA MASHAYACH AND THEIR MAYAPATA (WONDERS/ MIRACLES) **All by THEMSELVES**! KAN! ALL PRAISES TO THE MOST HIGH POWER* /ENERGY OF THE UNIVERSE!

I may not have the phantom rolls-royce I don't need, or what babylon amerika calls "riches" but I sure have a lot of "I Remember Whens!" Im so thankful and grateful for all My needs and desires that THE MOST HIGH has met and done for Me since My awakening! For starters, I remember when AHAYAH HIMSELF literally woke Me up to HIS/Our Truth early one Autumn morning in 2016 at approximately 1:30am. I heard THE MOST HIGH tell Me to get up and go look this Scripture up (starting with Deuteronomy 28) and to look that up on the internet the next morning around the same time. If not for HIS LOVE, I would still be in bondage to religion, bound up in the hypocritical church somewhere still thinking I was right about Salvation. ALL PRAISES FOR HIS COMPLETE RESCUE!

I remember a time when someone was ill and AHYAH led Me to Pray for them and they were healed. I remember when someone called Me to a hospital to pray for a baby girl in the Newborn Intensive Care Unit whom the doctors didn't expect to live long. Her family, Whom I'd never met before, looked so loving yet so frail and scared. I remember how AHAYAH touched that precious baby and the

46

last time I saw her they were celebrating her 10^h birthday. ALL PRAISES! I remember a time AHAYAH sent at least 4 different women to Me that were pregnant and contemplating abortion. By the time AHAYAH AHLAHAYAM finished using Me to counsel and minister to them, THE QADASH RAWACH had touched their hearts **_NOT_** to follow that wicked star of molach and remphan spoken **against** in Leviticus 18:21, Leviticus 20:2-5 and Acts 7:43 (some call it the star of David or shield of Solomon. That is nowhere in Scripture) to murder their children. Those Yisraelite Babies grew up to be, under AHAYAH, of course, the Pure Love and Happiness of those Women's lives! I remember when AHAYAH Delivered Me from transgressive habits that I had been taught were ok! HALALA! There's SO MANY, MANY Blessings and Miracles I could jot down here but as Yachaanah/John 21:25 Says, "***And there are also MANY OTHER THINGS that YASHA did, that, if They should be written every one, I suppose that even the world itself could not contain the books that should be written. KAN.***"

47

CHAPTER 9

ט

Psalm 150

This Tahaliyam needs NO commentary!

PRAISE Ye YASHA. PRAISE AHAYAH AHLAHAYAM in HIS Sanctuary: PRAISE HIM in the firmament of HIS POWER.

PRAISE HIM for HIS MIGHTY ACTS: Praise HIM according to HIS EXCELLENT Greatness.

PRAISE HIM with the Sound of The SHAFARA/Trumpet: PRAISE HIM with the psaltery and harp.

PRAISE HIM with the timbrel and dance: PRAISE HIM with stringed instruments and organs.

PRAISE HIM upon the loud cymbals: PRAISE HIM upon the high sounding cymbals.

LET EVERYTHING that hath breath PRAISE YASHA. PRAISE Ye YASHA!

ı

HE TURNED OUR CAPTIVITY!

YAHKAHAZAQAL/EZEKIEL 39:21-29

By now, due to AHAYAH AHLAHAYAM waking up **HIS TRUE PEOPLE** BY THE MASSES all across HIS very Rich Earth, Everyone knows or is learning *exactly* Who The 12 Sons of Yawachaab and True Yisraelites of The Scriptures Really Are. We Are learning and have learned that The Very Real and Very Much Alive People of The Scripture Are the so-called Black, African-american, Negro in america and across The Earth are actually **HA MASHAYACH'S Bloodline Descendants and Tribe of AHAYAH AHLAHAYAM AHLAHAYAM YAHAWADAH/YUDAH/JUDAH! HALALA!** The so-called Jamaican Are the Tribe Of Banyahman/Benyahman; *also* among Them are Yudah and some of Lawi/Leviites. The so-called Haitians are actually The Tribe of Lawi/Levi; The True Priests of AHAYAH. **We *Are* The True Chosen, Royal Seed Of THE MOST HIGH,** and make up the Southern Kingdom Of Yahsharalah/Yisrael by Blood. The Northern Kingdom, Who Are the rest of The Tribes of Yahsharalah, spoken of in 1 Kings 11 Is **scattered** predominately throughout Western and Southern Africa, but are also across The Earth. This is why there is no such thing as "spiritual Yisraelite/Hebrew" or a "messianic jew." Those are caucasian, demonically influenced, man-made, religious insults and mislabels, intended to insult AHAYAH and cause confusion so **HIS TRUE PEOPLE would forget Who and WHOSE We Truly Are! Yet, BY THE POWER OF AHAYAH AHLAHAYAM AND HIS SPIRIT QADASH RAWACH** THAT Leads, Guides and Comforts **Us FOREVER, WA THE BLOOD OF HIS SON YASHA HA MASHAYACH** That Covers Us **NOW AND FOREVER**, it didn't work!

ALL PRAISES TO THE MOST HIGH POWER!! We, Who've endured the curses of Deuteronomy   28 in the Diaspora for the past 400+ years as Slaves to Our enemies for disobeying AHAYAH'S COMMANDMENTS, Are The Very Real and **Natural** People of The Earth, now know **Exactly** Whose and Who We ARE! All Praises!

Many, Many people of other nations Scripturally known as heathens, and many gentiles, are finally waking up to the fact that they have been mistreating **THE MOST HIGH POWER'S TRUE CHOSEN SEED** and are feeling fear, shame, guilt, and some even show remorse for their wicked deeds against **HIS TRUE Children**. Hence, the curses that were once upon Us for disHonoring AHAYAH AHLAHAYAM THE MOST HIGH POWER, is now being reversed onto them **forever**. It is happening even now while people sleep. While they are awake. While they are at work, in the grocery store, so-called church, traveling from country to country, city to city, this awakening is happening! Praise **THE MOST HIGH** ALL MIGHTY! Everyday, The Awakening of Who True Yisrael IS and the curse reversal on Our enemies is happening and **cannot** nor will be stopped because it's too late! ALL PRAISES! The heathen chose to continue doing wrong against AHAYAH'S SEED when they had **many** chances and opportunities to do Right by AHAYAH and Us!

AHAYAH IS Demonstrating **HIS RULERSHIP** so, ALL you false, money-hungry, theiving, lying pastors, prophets, teachers, evangelists, preachers, politicians, so-called public figures, etc., **BEWARE!** **YOUR JUDGMENT IS SET! TRUE REPENTANCE IS KEY, HEBREW Yisraelites SCATTERED TO THE FOUR CORNERS OF THE EARTH! AHAYAH HAS NOT DONE AWAY WITH ***_HIS OWN_*** LAWS, STATUTES OR COMMANDMENTS OR HIS TRUE PEOPLE AS MALACHI 3:6 MAKES PLAIN! _"For I AM AHAYAH AHLAHAYAM AHLAHAYAM, ***I CHANGE NOT***; therefore Ye Sons of YACHAAB Are NOT consumed."KAN! HALALA! THERE ARE NOT JUST 10 COMMANDMENTS AS THE SO-CALLED "SUNDAY SCHOOL" TEACHERS MISLEAD US TO BELIEVE THERE WERE. THERE ARE ACTUALLY MANY, MANY MORE! YA'D BETTA WAKE UP AND DO THE RESEARCH AND STUDYING FOR YOURSELF LIKE 2 TIMOTHY 2:15 TEACHES**

US TO, "*STUDY to shew THYSELF APPROVED TO AHAYAH AHLAHAYAM, A Workman (or Woman) Who needeth NOT to be ashamed, RIGHTLY dividing THE WORD OF TRUTH.*" HURRY BECAUSE WE'RE ALMOST OUTTA TIME! YAH'S JUDGMENT IS ALREADY HERE ON THE EARTH RIGHT NOW AS WE SPEAK!

"*And I WILL set MY HONOR/SPLENDOR (glory) among the heathen (ANYONE that is not True Yisrael by Blood), and all the heathen shall see MY RULERSHIP (judgment) that I have executed, and MY HAND that I have laid upon them.*

So THE HOUSE OF Yisrael shall know that I BE AHAYAH AHLAHAYAM THEIR POWER/STRENGTH/ENERGY from that day and forward.

And the heathen shall know that THE HOUSE OF Yisrael went into captivity for Their iniquity: because They trespassed against ME, therefore hid I MY FACE from Them, and gave Them into the hand of Their enemies: so fell They all by the sword.

According to Their uncleanness and according to Their transgressions have I done to Them, and hid MY FACE from Them.

Therefore thus Saith AHAYAH AHLAHAYAM

POWER; NOW WILL I bring AGAIN the captivity of YACHAAB/Jacob, and have mercy upon THE WHOLE HOUSE OF Yisrael, and will be jealous for MY QADASH/SET APART (holy) NAME;

"After that They have borne Their shame, and ALL Their trespasses whereby They have trespassed against ME, when They dwelt safely in Their Land, and NONE made Them afraid.

When I HAVE brought Them AGAIN FROM the people, and GATHERED Them OUT of Their enemies' lands, and AM SET APART/Sanctified in Them in the sight of many nations;

Then shall They KNOW that I AM AHAYAH AHLAHAYAM Their POWER/ENERGY/STRENGTH, WHO caused Them TO BE LED into captivity among the heathen: BUT I HAVE GATHERED THEM to Their OWN LAND, and have left NONE of Them ANY MORE there.

Neither will I hide MY FACE ANY MORE from Them: for I HAVE poured out MY Rawach/SPIRIT upon THE HOUSE OF Yisrael SAITH AHAYAH AHLAHAYAM POWER."

SOON, EVERYONE WILL KNOW THE TRUTH! AHAYAH BE TRUTH! BARAKATHAW BE HE! BLESSED BE HE!

CHAPTER 11

ר

CLAP YOUR HANDS, TRUE MELANATED Yisrael!

"O CLAP YOUR HANDS, all Ye People; SHOUT to AHAYAH AHLAHAYAM with The Voice Of Triumph."

Psalm 47

Clapping Our Hands in Praise to **THE MOST HIGH** is a sonic BOOM in the ears of Our enemies, TAZAYAN!

How much of it do You think he or his serpent seed can listen to before having NO choice but to flee?!

O clap your hands, ALL Ye People; SHOUT to AHAYAH AHLAHAYAM with The Voice Of Triumph.

For AHAYAH AHLAHAYAM IS IRAWATAZA (TERRIBLE, OPPRESSOR, MIGHTY, POWER, STRONG, VIOLENT) (Hmm.. no wonder the wicked "speak non-violence" yet they are the most subtle, vial violent people on the earth against AHAYAH'S Righteousness People); HE IS A GREAT MALAK (KING) over ALL The Earth.

HE Shall subdue the people under Us, and the

nations under Our Feet.

HE Shall CHOOSE OUR INHERITANCE FOR US, The Excellency of Yachaab Whom HE HONORED (loved). Selah.

YASHA TAZABAAT IS gone up with a shout, HA MALAK with the sound of a SHAFARA/trumpet.

SING PRAISES TO AHAYAH AHLAHAYAM, SING PRAISES: SING PRAISES to OUR KING, SING PRAISES.

For AHAYAH IS THE KING OF ALL THE EARTH: SING Ye PRAISES with UNDERSTANDING.

AHAYAH AHLAHAYAM REIGNETH OVER the heathen: AHAYAH SITTETH UPON THE THRONE OF HIS QADASHNESS/SET APARTNESS.

The Princes of The People Are Gathered Together, even THE PEOPLE OF THE POWER OF Ahbaraham: for The Shields of The Earth Belong to AHAYAH AHLAHAYAM: HE IS GREATLY EXALTED!

TAZAYAN, Praise from YAHAWADAH IS not only an outward act. It's Who We Are as A People, A Tribe, a Nation. It is Our Lifestyle. Our Culture. Our Way of Life. We Were Preselected with This Special Gift of Praise To and For AHAYAH AHLAHAYAM ONLY.

I HAVE set Watchmen upon Thy Walls, O YARASHALIYAM/Yerusalem, Who shall NEVER hold Their SHALAWAM/Peace day nor night: Ye Who make mention of YASHA, keep not silence,

*****And GIVE HIM NO REST, till HE establish, and TILL HE MAKE YARASHALIYAM/ Yerusalem A PRAISE IN THE EARTH.******

YASHA HATH sworn by HIS RIGHT HAND, and by THE ARM OF HIS STRENGTH, Surely I WILL NO MORE give Thy corn to be meat for Thine enemies; and the sons of the stranger shall NOT drink Thy wine, for that that Thou hast laboured:

But They That have gathered it shall eat it, AND PRAISE AHAYAH AHLAHAYAM; and They That have brought it together shall drink it in THE COURTS OF MY QADASHNESS.

Go through, go through the gates; PREPARE Ye The Way of The (Yisraelite) People; cast up, cast up the highway; gather out the stones; lift up a standard for The People.

Behold, AHAYAH AHLAHAYAM hath proclaimed to the end of the world, Say ye to The Daughter of TAZAYAN, Behold, Thy Salvation cometh; behold, HIS REWARD IS WITH HIM, and His Work before HIM." YASHA 62:6-11

Who is like to THEE, O POWER, among the powers? who is like THEE, HONORABLE (glorious) in QADASHNESS- SET/APARTNESS (holiness), YARA-AH (fearful) in PRAISES, DOING WONDERS?

THOU STRETCHEDST OUT THY RIGHT HAND, The Earth swallowed them.

THOU IN THY Mercy hast led forth The People Whom THOU HAST REDEEMED: THOU HAST GUIDED THEM IN THY STRENGTH to THY QADASH/SET APART (holy) HABITATION.

The people shall hear, and be afraid: sorrow shall take hold on the inhabitants of palestina.

Then the dukes of edom shall be amazed; the mighty men of moab, trembling shall take hold upon them; ALL the inhabitants of canaan shall melt away.

Fear and dread shall fall upon them; BY THE GREATNESS OF THINE ARM they shall be as still as a stone; TILL THY PEOPLE PASS OVER, O AHAYAH AHLAHAYAM TILL THE PEOPLE PASS OVER, WHOM THOU HAST PURCHASED!

THOU SHALT BRING THEM IN, AND PLANT THEM IN THE MOUNTAIN OF THINE INHERITANCE, in The Place, O AHAYAH, WHOM THOU HAST MADE FOR THEE TO DWELL IN, in The Sanctuary, O KING, WHOM THY HANDS HAVE ESTABLISHED.

YASHA MASHAYACH SHALL REIGN FOR EVER AND EVER.

For the horse of pharaoh went in with his chariots and with his horsemen into the sea, and AHAYAH AHLAHAYAM BROUGHT AGAIN the waters of the sea upon them; *BUT THE CHILDREN OF Yisrael WENT ON DRY LAND IN THE MIDST OF THE SEA.

And Miriam The Prophetess, The Sister of Aaron, took a timbrel in Her Hand; and ALL The (Yisraelite) Women went out after Her with timbrels and with dances.

And Miriam answered Them, SING YE TO AHAYAH AHLAHAYAM, FOR HE HATH TRIUMPHED HONORABLY/VALIANTLY (gloriously); the horse and his rider HATH HE THROWN INTO THE SEA!"

EXODUS 15:10-21

AHAYAH IS ABOUT TO DO IT AGAIN FOR WE HIS TRUE PEOPLE YAHSHARALAH/Yisrael!!! WATCH OUT, NOW!!! KAN!!!

Let All the Natural Creation of AHAYAH AHLAHAYAM; Yisraelite Children, trees, birds, Plants, Animals, and every naturally living thing PRAISE AHAYAH AHLAHAYAM FOR HE BE ALL POWERFUL!

CHAPTER 12

ל

"But THOU ART QADASH/SET APART (holy), O THOU WHO INHABITEST The Praises of Yisrael."
Proverbs 22:3

Inhabit. **SHAKANA ESTEEM.** Dwell/Dwelling. To stay or sit in one location. Dwell, abide, remain, inhabit, rest, set, continue, Dweller. This is the Hebraic meaning of "Inhabit" per The Ancient Paleo Hebrew Lexicon #2838. Now, who in their right mind would not desire THE VERY **PRESENCE OF AHAYAH** TO INHABIT THEM OR THEIR DWELLING PLACE? I KNOW I DO!!

What happens when **AHAYAH'S** Presence IS in the room with You? I tell you The Truth, Healing happens. Deliverance Happens, Shalawam/Peace Happens, demons tremble, bow before **HIM** *and* flee! Miracles Happen. Whatever We need from **THE MOST HIGH** IS Ours! Praise brings clarity to the mind! It brings another level of focus and innerstanding of WHO **AHAYAH AHLAHAYAM BE! Praise gives You confidence in WHO THE MOST HIGH really BE!** Praise knocks down the fortress of the adversary! PRAISES TO AHAYAH WILL KEEP HIS SEED ALIVE, STRONG AND SAFE!
AHAYAH INHABITS The PRAISES of HIS

TRUE PEOPLE YAHSHARALAH!

What a POWERFUL image I see in My Mind! PRAISE AHBA AHAYAH! As I Praise and Worship AHBA AHAYAH AHLAHAYAM, the More HE comes into My life and believe Me, HE CAN HANDLE IT! BETTER THAN WE Humans and certainly others! Our MASTER IS ALSO OUR AHBA AND AH-HAB/FRIEND!

Remember Our enemies at yarachaa/jericho? Well, AHAYAH AHLAHAYAM IS DOING IT AGAIN! Just as HE did in Yahshawah 6:1-24

__But AS IT IS WRITTEN, Eye hath not seen, nor ear heard, neither have entered into the heart of (The Yisraelite) Man, the things that AHAYAH AHLAHAYAM HATH PREPARED for Them (The Awakened True Yisraelite) Who HONOR/RESPECT-love HIM!" 1 Corinthians 2:9__

"Allegedly" 1st documented Hebrew Yisraelite slave stepped foot off the first slave ship called the j.c. owned by a so-called "jew." His Royal foot touched the stolen and polluted soil in jamestown, virginia on August 20, 1619! Today is August 30, 2019! This will mean Our AHAYAH-inflicted punishment for breaking HIS Laws, Statutes and Commandments IS OVER! HALALA!

DURING THIS DELIVERANCE PERIOD, AHAYAH WILL REFINE US AND STRIKE HIS CURSES ONTO THOSE WHO HATE

HIM AND WE HIS PEOPLE; ALONG WITH
THOSE WHO'VE BENEFITED FROM THAT
HATRED.
HE IS SETTING HIS CAPTIVES FREE!
HALALA!
AHAYAH BARAK/BLESS US TO ENDURE
TO THE END

WITH <u>ALL</u> HELP FROM RAWACH HA
QADASH;

BECAUSE

AHAYAH TRULY *HAS* TURNED OUR
CAPTIVITY! EVEN THE CURSES ARE
BACK ONTO OUR ENEMIES AND ITS JUST
BEGINNING! HE IS DELIVERING WE HIS
NATION WITH HIS <u>MANY</u> GREAT SIGNS
AND WONDERS!

HALALA!

CHAPTER 13

□

A LAND FLOWING WITH MILK AND HONEY

Moreover AHAYAH Said, I am The STRENGTH of Thy Father, The POWER of Ahbaraham, The ENERGY of Yisaac, and The FORCE of Yachaab. And Masha hid His Face; for He was afraid to look upon AHAYAH.
And AHAYAH AHLAHAYAM Said, I HAVE SURELYseen the affliction of MY People Who Are in america/egypt, and HAVE HEARD THEIR CRY by reason of Their taskmasters; for I KNOW THEIR SORROWS;
And *I AM COME DOWN TO DELIVER THEM OUT of the hand of the americans/egyptians, AND TO BRING THEM UP out of that land (Yisrael) to a Right/good Land and a large, TO *A LAND FLOWING WITH MILK AND HONEY; to the place of the chaanaanites, and the hittites, and the amorites, and the perizzites, and the hivites, and the jebusites.
Now therefore, behold, THE CRY OF THE CHILDREN OF Yisrael IS COME TO ME: and I HAVE ALSO SEEN the oppression wherewith the americons/egyptians oppress Them.
Exodus 3:6-9

Lets get ready to leave babylon, yall! Lets obey Jeremiyah 50:6, 51:46; and Revelation 18:4.

HALALA!